Learning to Pray with St. Josemaría

Learning to Pray

with

St. Josemaría

Compiled by
Tom McDonough

Clemency Press

"Man attains to the merciful love of God, His mercy, to the extent that he himself is interiorly transformed in the spirit of that love towards his neighbor."
St. John Paul II, Dives in Misericordia, No. 14

Learning to Pray with St. Josemaría

Published by Clemency Press, Washington, D.C. 20016
www.clemencypress.com

ISBN # 978-0-9915788-3-2

Library of Congress Control Number: 2014945821

Acknowledgements:

The passages from St. Josemaría's writings were taken from escrivaworks.org with the permission of the copyright holder, Fundación Studium, Madrid, Spain. All rights reserved.

The photograph from on page 45 is used with the permission of Istituto Storico San Josemaría Escrivá, Rome, Italy. All rights reserved.

New Testament quotations are from *The Revised Standard Version of the Bible: Catholic Edition*, copyright © 1965, 1966 the Division of Christian Education of the National Council of the Churches of Christ in the United States of America. Used by permission. All rights reserved.

Cover Design: Tom McDonough

Cover Painting: Salvador "Boro" Perez, Courtesy of Universitní Centrum Na Baště, Prague, Czech Republic

Stay in touch with Clemency Press:

Follow us on Twitter: @ClemencyPress
Blog: Precursors of the Spirit of Pope Francis

Learning to Pray with St. Josemaría

Table of Contents

Introduction

The theme of my prayer is the theme of my life.

Christ is Passing By, No. 174

"Lord, teach us to pray."[1] The Apostles were fortunate enough to ask this question of the One who is Perfect God and Perfect Man, who gave us the most perfect prayer, the Our Father. We do well to repeat its words often, reflecting on Jesus' desire to leave us this prayer and meditating on it as the Apostles must have done for the rest of their lives.

We need even more help than the Apostles. We are poor students who need a good teacher. From his mid-teens, St. Josemaría Escrivá de Balaguer,[2]the founder of Opus Dei, engaged in a dialogue with the three persons of the Holy Trinity in an ever increasing intimacy. This was a conversation about the drama of the Will of God: what God wanted from him and the generosity of his response to what God asked.

St. Josemaría's preaching and writing projected his own prayer and reflection on Scripture and he encouraged those listening to him – people fully engaged in human activities – to pray in a similar manner: childlike, confident, rooted in the Gospels. Never, however, did he seek to pass on a particular method of prayer. He didn't want those following him to fall into routine imitation. He wanted to leave them open to use their own freedom in response to the inspirations of the Holy Spirit.

> In the presence of the Triune God, invoking Mary as our mediatrix and beseeching St. Joseph, our father and lord, to be our advocate, we will speak of our everyday work,

[1] Luke 11, 1

[2] For more information on St. Josemaría, go to http://opusdei.org/en/section/biography-2/. Accessed August 4, 2014.

> of our family, of our friendships, of our big plans and little shortcomings.[3]

This book presents St. Josemaría's prayer in two ways. Part I takes selections from his written works in which he interrupts his preaching or writing in order to speak directly with God.

Part II is his collection of New Testament passages assembled in 1933 for his own prayer, reflection and preaching.[4]

Together, they accent the simple, confident, childlike way he talked to his divine Father. Together, they set us on that quest St. Josemaría proposed to each one of us:

> May you seek Christ,
> May you find Christ,
> May you love Christ.
>
> *The Way, No. 382*

St. Josemaría's message was and is that God calls us all to holiness in the midst of the mundane things of every day. He invites us to converse with Him right there. This was new. It still is new for many people.

> You write: 'To pray is to talk with God. But about what?' About what? About Him, about yourself: joys, sorrows, successes and failures, noble ambitions, daily worries, weaknesses! And acts of thanksgiving and petitions: and Love and reparation.
>
> In a word: to get to know him and to get to know yourself: 'to get acquainted!'.[5]

---

[3] CHRIST IS PASSING BY, No.174.

[4] Varo, Francisco, *San Josemaría Escriva de Balaguer, "Palabras del Nuevo Testamento, repetidas veces meditadas, Junio – 1933,"* Studia et Documenta, Vol. 1, 2007, pp. 259-286.

So, go ahead. "Open your own hearts and tell Jesus your story."[6]

---

[5] THE WAY, No. 91.
[6] CHRIST IS PASSING BY, No. 1.

Part I

Tell Him…

Tell Him…

> Ask your Mother Mary, ask Saint Joseph and your Guardian Angel to speak to the Lord and tell him the things you can't manage to put into words because you are so dull.
>
> *The Forge,* No. 272

We certainly are dull and a bit dim-witted. St. Josemaría makes praying seem easy and perhaps we feel a tinge of envy of his ability to pray. With the help of the Holy Spirit he was able to draw great insights from prayers we say every day.

> I often had the custom, when I was young, of not using any book when making a meditation. I would recite, savoring them, the words of the Our Father, and, I would pause, relishing the thought, when I considered that God is Father, my Father, and that this makes me a brother of Jesus Christ and a brother to all people. I never got over my astonishment, contemplating that I was a son of God! After each reflection I found myself firmer in faith, more secure in hope, more on fire with love.[7]

In his personal notes he often recorded the very words of his dialogue with God. Many of these notes found their way into his published works where we find him turning from the reader to Our Lord or Our Lady and addressing them personally or sometimes inviting us to "Tell Him this…" or "Say to Him…"

These flights of prayer are marked in **bold**, sometime with accompanying text for clarity. They are instructive for our own prayer. We can follow his example. Some will help our own prayer find expression, others can be adopted as aspirations to be repeated frequently during the day. But we should not just repeat

---

[7] St. Josemaria Escriva, Letter, 8 December, 1949, no. 41, in Andres Vazquez de Prada, THE FOUNDER OF OPUS DEI, Vol I, Princeton, N.J., Scepter, 2001, p. 308.

the words. We can make them our own by putting our hearts and minds into them.

Bold Love

> The holiness we should be striving for is… a charity that is to be practiced exactly as our Lord himself commands: "Thou shalt love the Lord thy God, with thy whole heart, and with thy whole soul and with thy whole mind," holding back nothing for ourselves. This is what sanctity is all about.
>
> *Friends of God*, No. 6

Jesus has given us a lofty goal, to love as he loved us. He who has given us the goal will give us the grace.

Lord, I really do want to be a saint. I really do want to be a worthy disciple of yours and to follow you unconditionally.

Friends of God, No.20

Lord, grant me the love with which you want me to love you.

Forge, No. 270

We belong to God completely, soul and body, flesh and bones, all our senses and faculties. Ask him, confidently: **Jesus, guard our hearts! Make them big and strong and tender, hearts that are affectionate and refined, overflowing with love for you and ready to serve all mankind.**

Friends of God, No. 177

My God, I love you, but... oh teach me to love!

The Way, No. 423

You say that you don't know how to pray? Put yourself in the presence of God, and once you have said, **Lord, I don't know how to pray!** rest assured that you have begun to do so.

The Way, No. 90

It hurts me to see the danger of lukewarmness in which you place yourself when you do not strive seriously for perfection in your state in life.

Say with me: **I don't want to be lukewarm! Pierce my flesh with your fear: grant me, my God, a filial fear that will make me react!**

The Way, No. 326

I had to smile at the impatience of your prayer. You were telling him: **I don't want to grow old, Jesus... To have to wait so long to see you! Then, perhaps I won't have a heart as inflamed as mine is now. "Then" seems too late. Now, my union would be more ardent for I love you now with the pure Love of youth.**

The Way, No. 111

Tell him: **Lord, I want nothing other than what You want. Even those things I am asking you for at present, if they take me an inch away from your Will, don't give them to me.**

The Forge, No. 512

Are things going against you? Are you going through a rough time? Say very slowly, as if relishing it, this powerful and manly prayer: **May the most just and most lovable will of God be done, be fulfilled be praised and eternally exalted above all things. Amen, Amen.** I assure you that you will find peace.

The Way, No. 691

Jesus, I don't want to think of what "tomorrow" will be like, for I don't want to put limits on your generosity.

The Forge, No. 1032

Jesus, may I be last in everything... and first in Love.

The Way, No. 430

Say slowly and in all earnestness: ***Nunc coepi*** **— now I begin!**

Don't get discouraged if, unfortunately, you don't see any great change in yourself brought about by the Lord's right hand... From your lowliness you can cry out: **Help me, my Jesus, because I want to fulfill your Will... your most lovable Will!**

The Forge, No. 398

How joyfully the holy guardian Angels must have obeyed that soul who said to them: **Holy Angels, I call on you, like the Spouse of the Song of Songs, to tell him that I languish with love.**

The Way, No. 568

Oh, Jesus! I rest in you.

The Way, No. 732

Lord, I ask for a gift from you: Love… a Love that will cleanse me. — And another gift as well: self-knowledge so that I may be filled with humility.

The Forge, No. 185

Abandonment to the will of God is the secret of happiness on earth. Say, then: **My food is to do his will.**

The Way, No. 766

Remove, Jesus, that filthy crust of sensual corruption which covers my heart, so that I can feel and readily follow the touches of the Paraclete on my soul.

The Way, No. 130

Don't hesitate: let your lips pronounce a heartfelt *Fiat,* **Be it done!**, which will be the crown of your sacrifice.

The Way, No. 763

Lord, why do you call it a new commandment? It was already laid down in the Old Testament that we should love our neighbour. You will remember also that, when Jesus had scarcely begun his public life, he broadened the scope of this law with divine generosity: 'You have heard that it was said, You shall love your neighbour and hate your enemy. But I tell you, Love your enemies, do good to those who hate you, pray for those who persecute and slander you.**But, Lord, please allow us to insist. Why do you still call this precept new? That night, just a few hours before offering yourself in sacrifice on the Cross, during your intimate conversation with the men who — in spite of being weak and wretched, like ourselves — accompanied you to Jerusalem, you revealed to us the standard for our charity, one we could never have suspected: 'as I have loved you'. How well the apostles must have understood you, having witnessed for themselves your unbounded love.**

Friends of God, No. 223

Jesus, whatever you 'want', I love!

The Way, No. 773

Good child, say to Jesus many times each day: **I love you, I love you, I love you...**

The Way, No. 878

My clumsiness, Beloved, is so great, so very great that even when I wish to caress I cause pain. Refine the manners of my soul: within the sturdy manliness of this life of childhood, give me — I want you to give me — the gentleness and affection that children show towards their parents in their intimate outpourings of love.

The Way, No. 883

What a wonderful thing it is to be a child! When a man asks a favor, his request must be backed by a list of his qualifications.

When it is a child who asks — since children haven't any qualifications — it's enough for him to say: I'm a son of So-and-so.

Ah, Lord, say it to him with all your heart!, **I am a son of God!**

The Way, No. 892

Have you seen the gratitude of little children? Imitate them, saying to Jesus, when things are favorable and when they are adverse: **How good you are! How good!**

These words, if you mean them, are the way of childhood, and will bring you peace, with due measure of tears and laughter, and without measure of Love.

The Way, No. 894

Our will, strengthened by grace, is all-powerful before God. If, for instance, as we travel in a bus, we are struck by the thought of so many offences against God and say to Jesus, backing our words with our will **My God, I wish I could make an act of love and reparation for every turn of the wheels carrying me,** in that very instant, in the eyes of Jesus, we really have loved him and atoned just as we desired.

The Way, No. 897

My God, teach me how to love! — My God, teach me how to pray!

The Forge, No. 66

Lord: may I have due measure in everything... except in Love.

The Way, No. 427

You should repeat very often: **Jesus, if ever a doubt creeps into my soul, setting up other noble ambitions in place of what you are asking of me, I tell you now that I prefer to follow you, no matter how much it costs. Do not leave me!**

The Forge, No. 292

My God, when am I going to convert?

The Forge, No. 112

In your prayer of spiritual childhood what childish things you say to your Lord! With the confidence of a child speaking to his great Friend of whose love he is utterly sure, you confided in him, saying, **May I live only for your Glory!**

The Forge, No. 353

Learn to praise the Father, the Son and the Holy Spirit. Learn to have a special devotion to the Blessed Trinity: **I believe in God the Father, I believe in God the Son, I believe in God the Holy Spirit; I hope in God the Father, I hope in God the Son, I hope in God the Holy Spirit; I love God the Father, I love God the Son, I love God the Holy Spirit. I believe, I hope and I love the most Holy Trinity.**

This devotion is much needed as a supernatural exercise for the soul, expressed by the movement of the heart, although not always in words.

The Forge, No. 296

Little child, say to Jesus: **I will not be satisfied with anything less than You.**

The Forge, No. 352

Lord, I will trust in you alone. Help me to be faithful to you. I know that I can look forward to everything as a result of being faithful in your service, abandoning all my cares and worries into your hands.

The Forge, No. 903

... as we begin this time of prayer close to the tabernacle, ask him, like the blind man in the Gospel did**, *Domine, ut videam*! Lord, that I may see! Enlighten my intelligence and let Christ's words penetrate deep into my mind. Strengthen his Life in my soul so that I may be transformed in readiness for eternal Glory.**

Friends of God, No. 127

From there, where you are working, let your heart escape to the Lord, right close to the Tabernacle, to tell him, without doing anything odd, **My Jesus, I love You.**

Don't be afraid to call him so — my Jesus — and to say it to him often.

The Forge, No. 746

Listen to me, my child: you must be happy when people treat you badly and dishonor you, when many come out against you excitedly and it becomes the done thing to spit on you, because you are like the refuse of the world.

It's hard, it's very hard. It is hard, until at last a man goes to the Tabernacle, seeing himself thought of as the scum of the earth, like a wretched worm, and says with all his heart **"Lord, if you don't need my good name, what do I want it for?"**

Up to then even that son of God does not know what happiness is — up to that point of nakedness and self-giving, which is a self-giving of love, but founded on mortification, on sorrow.

The Forge, No. 803

My God, when will I love you for yourself? Although when we think about it, Lord, to desire an everlasting reward is to desire you, for you give yourself as our reward.

The Forge, No. 1030

Say to him: **Here I am, for you have called me!**

The Way, No. 984

The Help of a Mother

> Love our Lady. And she will obtain for you abundant grace to conquer in your daily struggle. And the enemy will gain nothing by those foul things that continually seem to boil and rise within you, trying to engulf in their fragrant corruption the high ideals, the sublime determination that Christ himself has set in your heart. — *Serviam*, I will serve!
>
> *The Way,* No. 493

Devotion to the Blessed Mother is always centered on Jesus, a fact well understood by St. Josemaría who didn't want to be imitated in anything except his devotion to Our Lady.

❧

Mother, do not leave me! Let me seek your Son, let me find your Son, let me love your Son — with my whole being!

Remember me, my Lady, remember me.

The Forge, No. 157

How people like to be reminded of their relationship with distinguished figures in literature, in politics, in the army, in the Church!... Sing to the Immaculate Virgin, reminding her: **Hail Mary, daughter of God the Father: Hail Mary, Mother of God the Son: Hail Mary, Spouse of God the holy Spirit... Greater than you, none but God!**

The Way, No. 496

Heavenly Mother, let me regain once more fervor, dedication, self-denial: in one word, Love.

The Forge, No. 162

Holy Mary, "Queen of Apostles," queen of all those who desire to make the love of your Son known, you understand our miseries so well. Ask Jesus' forgiveness for our shabby lives — for what could have been fire and has been ashes, for the lights that have gone out, for the salt that has turned insipid.

Christ is Passing By, No. 175

Say to her: **Mother, my Mother,** yours, because you are hers on many counts, **may your love bind me to your Son's Cross: may I not lack the Faith, nor the courage, nor the daring, to carry out the will of our Jesus.**

The Way, No. 497

Mother, Oh Mother! With that word of yours — *fiat*, be it done — you have made us brothers of God and heirs to his Glory. Blessed art thou!

The Way, No. 512

Mother of God, you are omnipotent in your petition. Obtain for us, along with forgiveness, the strength to live truly a life of faith and love, so we can share our faith in Christ with others.

Christ is Passing By, No. 175

Most Sweet Heart of Mary, prepare a safe way. Guide our steps on earth with strength and security. Become for us the path we are to follow, since you in your love know the way, a sure short-cut, to the love of Jesus Christ.

Christ is Passing By, No. 178

Turn to Our Lady and ask her, as a token of her love for you, for the gift of contrition. Ask that you may be sorry, with the sorrow of Love, for all your sins and for the sins of all men and women throughout the ages.

And with that same disposition, be bold enough to add: **Mother, my life, my hope, lead me by the hand... And if there is anything in me which is displeasing to my Father God grant that I may see it, so that, between the two of us, we may uproot it.**

Do not be afraid to continue: **O clement, O loving, O sweet Virgin Mary, pray for me, that by fulfilling the most lovable Will of your Son, I may be worthy to obtain and enjoy what Our Lord Jesus has promised.**

The Forge, No. 161

My Mother! Mothers on earth look with greater love on the weakest of their children, the one with the worst health, or who is least intelligent, or is a poor cripple...**—Sweet Lady! I know that you are more of a Mother than all other mothers put together. — And, since I am your son... And, since I am weak, and ill... and crippled... and ugly...**

The Forge, No. 234

Mary, the holy Mother of our king, the queen of our heart, looks after us as only she knows how. **Mother of mercy, throne of grace: we ask you to help us compose, verse by verse, the simple poem of charity in our own life and the lives of the people around us; it is "like a river of peace." For you are a sea of inexhaustible mercy: "All streams run to the sea, but the sea is never full."**

Christ is Passing By, No. 187

It is impossible to live a clean life without God's help. God wants us to be humble, and to ask him for his help through our Mother who is his Mother.

You should say to Our Lady, right now, speaking without the sound of words, from the accompanied solitude of your heart: **O, my Mother, sometimes this poor heart of mine rebels... But if you help me.**

She will indeed help you to keep it clean and to follow the way God has called you to pursue. The Virgin Mary will always make it easier for you to fulfill the Will of God.

The Forge, No. 315

Dear Lady, Mother of God and my Mother, not in the remotest way do I wish that you may ever be anything less than Mistress and Empress of the whole of creation.

The Forge, No. 376

Holy Mary, Star of the sea, be our guide. Make this firm request, because there is no storm which can shipwreck the most Sweet Heart of Mary. When you see the storm coming, if you get into that firm Refuge which is Mary, there will be no danger of your wavering or going down.

The Forge, No. 1055

Trustingly beg Our Lady, as you accompany her in the solitude of your heart, without saying anything out loud: **Mother, this poor heart of mine rebels so foolishly... If you don't protect me...** And she will help you to keep it pure and to follow the way to which God has called you.

Friends of God, No. 180

The Perennial Puzzle

Is it not true that as soon as you cease to be afraid of the Cross, of what people call the cross, when you set your will to accept the Will of God, then you find happiness, and all your worries, all your sufferings, physical or moral, pass away?

Truly the Cross of Jesus is gentle and lovable. There, sorrows cease to count; there is only the joy of knowing that we are co-redeemers with Him.

The Way of the Cross, Station 2

"The idea of expiation is incomprehensible to the modern mind."[8] Perhaps, if I ask hard enough, Jesus will take away my modern mind and give me a mind like His own.

ഩഌ❦✿❦ഩഌ

'If any man has a mind to come my way, let him renounce self, and take up his cross, and follow me.' That is why I like to ask Jesus, for myself, **Lord, no day without a cross!** Then, through God's grace, our characters will grow strong and we will become a point of support for our God, over and above our own wretchedness.

Friends of God, No. 216

Lord, if it is your will, turn my poor flesh into a Crucifix.

The Way, No. 775

To have the Cross is to have found happiness: it is to have you, Lord!

The Forge, No. 766

---

[8] Ratzinger, Joseph, Pope Benedict XVI, JESUS OF NAZARETH, Part Two, San Francisco, Ignatius Press, 2011, p. 119.

To save mankind, Lord, you died on the Cross. And yet for one mortal sin you condemn a man to a hapless eternity of suffering. How much sin must offend you, and how much I ought to hate it!

The Forge, No. 1002

Show him again that you really want to be his. **O Jesus, help me. Make me really yours; may I burn and be consumed, by dint of little things that no one notices.**

The Forge, No. 620

Jesus, compared to your Cross, of what value is mine? Alongside your wounds, what are my little scratches? Compared with your Love, so immense and pure and infinite, of what value is this tiny little sorrow which you have placed upon my shoulders?

Friends of God, No. 310

Custody of the heart. That priest used to pray: **Jesus, may my poor heart be an enclosed garden; may my poor heart be a paradise where you live; may my Guardian Angel watch over it with a sword of fire and use it to purify every affection before it comes into me. Jesus, with the divine seal of your Cross, seal my poor heart.**

The Forge, No. 412

My God, how is it that I do not cry out in sorrow and love whenever I see a Crucifix?

The Forge, No. 29

Grant me, Jesus, the Cross with no Simon of Cyrene to help me. No, that's not right; I need your grace, I need your help here as in everything. You must be my Simon of Cyrene. With you, my God, no trial can daunt me…

But what if my Cross should consist in boredom or sadness?

In that case I say to you, Lord, with You I would gladly be sad.

The Forge, No. 252

The Cross, the Holy Cross, is heavy.

First there are my sins. Then the sad truth of our Mother the Church's suffering; the apathy of so many Catholics who want without really wanting; the separation, for all kinds of reasons, from those we love; the sufferings and trials of ourselves and of others. The Cross, the Holy Cross, is heavy.

May the most just, the most lovable Will of God be done, be fulfilled, be praised and exalted above all things for ever! Amen. Amen.

The Forge, No. 769

Lord, fill me with your clarity, make me share in your divinity so that I may identify my will with your adorable Will and become the instrument you wish me to be. Give me the madness of the humiliation you underwent, which led you to be born poor, to work in obscurity, to the shame of dying sewn with nails to a piece of wood, to your self-effacement in the Blessed Sacrament.

Furrow, No. 273

Now, when the Cross has become a serious and weighty matter, Jesus will see to it that we are filled with peace. He will become our Simon of Cyrene, to lighten the load for us.

Then say to him, trustingly: **Lord, what kind of a Cross is this? A Cross which is no cross. Now I know the trick. It is to abandon myself in you; and from now on, with your help, all my crosses will always be like this.**

The Forge, No. 764

My Wretchedness

> Experience of sin should not make us doubt our mission.... Christ gives us his risen life, he rises in us, if we become sharers in his cross and his death.... Not so much despite our wretchedness but in some way through it.... Christ is shown forth: in our effort to be better, to have a love which wants to be pure, to overcome our selfishness, to give ourselves fully to others, to turn our existence into a continuous service.
>
> *Christ is Passing By,* No. 114

My wretchedness could tempt me to withdraw from God out of shame or discouragement. St. Josemaría recommends just the opposite: The awareness of our defects must bring us closer to God who is all-merciful. From here, from rockbottom, I have a new chance of approaching God with humility and repentance.

Lord, take away my pride; crush my self-love, my desire to affirm myself and impose myself on others. Make the foundation of my personality my identification with you.

Christ is Passing By, No. 31

You were saying to him: **You mustn't trust me. But I..., I do trust you, Jesus. I abandon myself in your arms: there I leave all that is mine, my weaknesses!** And I think it is a good prayer.

The Way, No. 113

Each day, my God, I am less sure of myself and more sure of you!

The Way, No. 729

Jesus, my Love, to think that I could offend you again! I am yours: save me!

The Forge, No. 196

When we are faced with weaknesses and sins, with our mistakes even though, by God's grace, they be of little account, let us turn to God our Father in prayer and say to him**, Lord, here I am in my wretchedness and frailty, a broken vessel of clay. Bind me together again, Lord, and then, helped by my sorrow and by your forgiveness, I shall be stronger and more attractive than before!** What a consoling prayer, which we can say every time something fractures this miserable clay of which we are made.

Friends of God, No. 95

Just now, Jesus, when I was considering my wretchedness, I said to you: Allow yourself to be taken in by this son of yours, just like those good fathers, full of kindness, who put into the hands of their little children the presents they want to receive from them... knowing perfectly well that little children have nothing of their own.

And what merriment of father and son, even though they are both in on the secret!

The Forge, No. 195

When human beings have work to do they try to use the right tools for the job. But when God wants to carry out some piece of work, he uses unsuitable means, so that it can be seen that the work is his. How often you have heard me say this!

So you and I, who are aware of the massive weight of our failings, should tell Our Lord: **Wretched as I am, I still understand that in your hands I am a divine instrument.**

The Forge, No. 610

Ask the Father, the Son and the Holy Spirit, and your Mother, to make you know yourself and weep for all those foul things that have passed through you, and which, alas, have left such dregs behind... — And at the same time, without wishing to stop considering all that, say to him: **Jesus, give me a Love that will act like a purifying fire in which my miserable flesh, my miserable heart, my miserable soul, my miserable body may be consumed and cleansed of all earthly wretchedness. And when I have been completely emptied of myself, fill me with yourself. May I never become attached to anything here below. May Love always sustain me.**

The Forge, No. 41

Put your head frequently round the oratory door to say to Jesus… **I abandon myself into your arms.** – Leave everything you have – your wretchedness – at his feet. – In this way, in spite of the welter of things you carry along behind you, you will never lose your peace.

The Forge, No. 306

O Jesus! If in spite of the poor way I have behaved, you have done for me what you have done..., what would you do if I were to respond well?

This truth will lead you to be generous without respite. Weep, and grieve with sorrow and love, for Our Lord and his Blessed Mother deserve different treatment from you.

The Forge, No. 388

Remember, Lord, the promises you made, filling me with hope; they console me in my nothingness and fill my life with strength.

Friends of God, No. 305

If you feel for whatever reason that you cannot manage, abandon yourself in God, telling him: **Lord, I trust in you, I abandon myself in you, but do help me in my weakness!**

And filled with confidence, repeat: **See Jesus what a filthy rag I am. My life seems to me so miserable. I am not worthy to be a son of yours.** Tell him all this — and tell him so over and over again.

It will not be long before you hear him say, *Do not be afraid* and also: *Rise up and walk*!

The Forge, No. 287

When you have fallen or when you find yourself overwhelmed by the weight of your wretchedness, repeat with a firm hope: **Lord, see how ill I am; Lord, you who died on the Cross for love of me, come and heal me.**

Be full of confidence, I insist. Keep on calling out to his most loving Heart. As he cured the lepers we read about in the Gospel, he will cure you.

The Forge, No. 213

Your prayer went like this: **My wretchedness weighs me down, but it doesn't overwhelm me because I am a son of God. I want to atone, to Love... And**, you added, **like Saint Paul, I want to turn my weaknesses to good use, convinced that the Lord will not abandon those who place their trust in him.**

Carry on like that. I assure you that, with God's grace, you will succeed, and you will overcome your wretchedness and your shortcomings.

The Forge, No. 294

When we're working for God we have to have a "superiority complex", I told you.

But isn't that a sign of pride? you asked me. No! It is a consequence of humility; the humility which makes me say: **Lord, you are who you are. I am nothingness itself. You have all the perfections: power, strength, love, glory, wisdom, authority, dignity... If I unite myself to you, like a child who goes to the strong arms of his father or the wonderful lap of his mother, I will feel the warmth of your divinity, I will feel the light of your wisdom, I will feel your strength coursing through my veins.**

The Forge, No. 342

Dear Jesus, I do want to correspond to your Love, but I am so feeble. With your grace, I will know how to!

The Forge, No. 383

Lord, rescue me from myself!

The Forge, No. 120

Today once again I prayed full of confidence. This was my petition: **Lord, may neither our past wretchedness which has been forgiven us, nor the possibility of future wretchedness cause us any disquiet. May we abandon ourselves into your merciful hands. May we bring before you our desires for sanctity and apostolate, which are hidden like embers under the ashes of an apparent coldness. Lord, I know you are listening to us.**

You should say this to him too.

The Forge, No. 426

Tell him: **Jesus, I cannot see a single perfect flower in my garden, all are blighted. It seems that all have lost their color and their scent. Poor me! Face downwards in the muck, on the ground: that's my place.**

That's the way, humble yourself. He will conquer in you, and you will attain the victory.

The Forge, No. 606

Our life, a Christian's life, has to be as ordinary as this: trying every day to do well those very things it is our duty to do; carrying out our divine mission in the world by fulfilling the little duty of each moment.

Or rather, struggling to fulfill it. Sometimes we don't manage, and when night comes, in our examination, we'll have to tell Our Lord, **I am not offering you virtues; today I can only offer you defects. But with your grace I will be able to count myself a victor.**

The Forge, No. 616

"Lord, if you will" — and you are always willing — "you can make me clean." You know my weaknesses; I feel these symptoms; I suffer from these failings. We show him the wound, with simplicity, and if the wound is festering, we show the pus too. **Lord, you have cured so many souls; help me to recognize you as the divine physician, when I have you in my heart or when I contemplate your presence in the tabernacle.**

Christ is Passing By, No. 93

You told me, in confidence, that in your prayer you would open your heart to God with these words: **I think of my wretchedness, which seems to be on the increase in spite of the graces you give me. It must be due to my failure to correspond. I know that I am completely unprepared for the enterprise you are asking of me. And when I read in the newspapers of so very many highly qualified and respected men, with talents and money, speaking, writing, organizing in defense of your reign... I look at myself, and see that I'm a nobody: ignorant, poor: so little, in a word. This would fill me with shame if I did not know that you want me to be so. But Lord Jesus, you know how very gladly I have put my ambition at your feet... To have Faith and Love, to be loving, believing, suffering. In these things I do want to be rich and learned: but no more rich or learned than you, in your limitless Mercy, have wanted me to be. I desire to put all my prestige and honor into fulfilling your most just and most lovable Will.**

I then said to you: don't let this remain merely as a good desire.

The Forge, No. 822

As we call to mind our infidelities, and so many mistakes, weaknesses, so much cowardice - each one of us has his own experience - let us repeat to Our Lord, from the bottom of our hearts, Peter's cry of contrition**, Lord, you know all things, you know that I love you, despite my wretchedness!** And I would even add**, You know that I love you, precisely because of my wretchedness, for it leads me to rely on you who are my strength: *quia tu es, Deus, fortitudo mea.***

And at that point let us start again.

Friends of God, No. 17

Faced with the marvels of God, and with all our human failures, we have to make this admission: **You are everything to me. Use me as you wish!**

Then there will be no more loneliness for you, for us.

The Forge, No. 751

My God, when I look at my own poor life, I find no reason to be vain and still less to be proud: all I see are abundant reasons why I should be always humble and contrite. I know full well that a life of service is man's noblest calling.

Friends of God, No. 309

A Divine Companion

We've got to be convinced that God is always near us. We live as though he were far away, in the heavens high above, and we forget that he is also continually by our side.

He is there like a loving Father. He loves each one of us more than all the mothers in the world can love their children — helping us, inspiring us, blessing... and forgiving.

We've got to be filled, to be imbued with the idea that our Father, and very much our Father, is God who is both near us and in heaven.

The Way, No. 267

Who would have guessed that God wants to be so close to us? Who would have guessed that God wants to accompany us every day on our life journey: whispering good advice, showing us how to behave, encouraging us to flourish in this life and the next?

Lord, give us your grace. Open the door to the workshop in Nazareth so that we may learn to contemplate you, together with your holy Mother Mary and the holy Patriarch St Joseph, whom I love and revere so dearly, the three of you dedicated to a life of work made holy. Then, Lord, our poor hearts will be enkindled, we shall seek you and find you in our daily work, which you want us to convert into a work of God, a labor of Love.

Friends of God, No. 72

My Lord Jesus, grant that I may feel your grace and second it in such a way that I empty my heart... so that you may fill it, my Friend, my Brother, my King, my God, my Love!

The Forge, No. 913

Jesus, if there is anything in me which is displeasing to you, tell me what it is so that we may uproot it.

The Forge, No. 108

Lord, why have you given us this power? Why have you entrusted us with the faculty of choosing you or rejecting you? You want us to make good use of this power. Lord, what you do want me to do? His reply is precise, crystal-clear: 'Thou shalt love the Lord thy God with thy whole heart and with thy whole soul and with thy whole mind.'

Friends of God, No. 27

Isn't it true, Lord, that you were greatly consoled by the childlike remark of that man who, when he felt the disconcerting effect of obedience in something unpleasant, whispered to you: 'Jesus, keep me smiling!'?

The Way, No. 626

Say slowly to the Master: **Lord, all I want is to serve you. All I want is to fulfill my duties and love you with all my heart. Make me feel your firm step by my side. May you be my only support!**

Say this to him slowly... and really mean it!

The Forge, No. 449

Cry aloud. for that cry is the folly of one in love: **Lord, even though I love you... don't trust me! Bind me to yourself, more closely every day!**

Furrow, No. 799

Let each of us, myself included, put our trust in Jesus, saying to him: **Lord, I am ready to struggle and I know that you do not lose battles. I realize too that if at times I lose, it is because I have gone away from you. Take me by the hand. Don't trust me. Don't let go of me.**

Friends of God, No. 183

Lord, from now on let me become someone else: no longer "me", but that "other person" you would like me to be.

Let me not deny you anything you ask of me. Let me know how to pray. Let me know how to suffer. Let me not worry about anything except your glory. Let me feel your presence all the time.

May I love the Father. May I hunger for you, my Jesus, in a permanent Communion. May the Holy Spirit set me on fire.

The Forge, No. 122

When you want to do things well, really well, it's then you do them worst. Humble yourself before Jesus, saying to him: **Don't you see how I do everything badly? Well, if you don't help me very much, I'll do it all even worse! Take pity on your child: you see, I want to write a big page each day in the book of my life. But, I'm so clumsy!; and if the Master doesn't guide my hand, instead of graceful strokes my pen leaves behind blots and scrawls that can't be shown to anyone. From now on, Jesus, we'll always do the writing together.**

The Way, No. 882

My God, I see I shall never accept you as my Savior unless I acknowledge you as my Model at the same time.

Since you yourself chose to be poor, make me love holy poverty. I resolve, with your grace, to live and die in poverty, even though I may have millions at my disposal.

The Forge, No. 46

It only takes a second. Before setting about anything, ask yourself: **What does God want of me in this?** Then, with divine grace, do it!

The Way, No. 778

We lack faith. The day we practice this virtue, trusting in God and in his Mother, we will be courageous and loyal. God, who is the same God as ever, will work miracles through our hands.

Grant me, dear Jesus, the faith I truly desire! My Mother, sweet Lady, Mary most holy, make me believe!

The Forge, No. 235

When you find yourself tired and exhausted, approach Our Lord confidently and say: **Jesus, see what you can do about it. Even before I begin to fight, I am already tired.**

He will give you his strength.

The Forge, No. 244

Today in your prayer you confirmed your resolution to be a saint. I understand you when you make this more specific by adding, **I know I shall succeed, not because I am sure of myself, Jesus, but because… I am sure of you.**

The Forge, No. 320

He was hungry. The Maker of the universe, the Lord of all creation, experiences hunger! **Thank you, Lord, for inspiring the sacred author to include this small touch here, a detail that makes me love you more and which encourages me to desire ardently to contemplate your sacred Humanity!** Perfect God and perfect Man, of flesh and bone, just like you and I.

Friends of God, No. 50

We should let Jesus know that we are children. And when children are tiny and innocent, what a lot of effort it takes for them to go up one step. They look as though they are wasting their time, but eventually they manage to climb up. Now there is another step. Crawling on their hands and knees, and putting their whole body into it, they score another success... one more step. Then they start again. What an effort! There are only a few more steps to go now... But then the toddler stumbles... and — whoops! — down he goes. With bumps all over and in floods of tears, the poor child sets out and begins to try again. **We are just like that, Jesus, when we are on our own. Please take us up in your loving arms, like a big and good Friend of the simple child. Do not leave us until we have reached the top. And then, oh then!, we will know how to correspond to your Merciful Love, with the daring of young children, telling you, sweet Lord, that after Mary and Joseph, there never has been nor will there ever be a mortal soul, and there have been some really crazy ones, who loves you as much as I love you.**

The Forge, No. 346

This is how you should pray: **If I am to do anything worthwhile, Jesus, you will have to do it for me. May your Will be done. I do love it, even if your Will should permit that I be always as I am now, falling dismally only to be lifted up by you!**

The Forge, No. 390

When you are troubled... and also in the hour of success, say again and again, **Lord, don't let go of me, don't leave me, help me as you would a clumsy child; always lead me by the hand!**

The Forge, No. 654

Continue thinking about the donkey's good qualities and notice how in order to do anything worth while, it has to allow itself to be ruled by the will of whoever is leading it... On its own the donkey would only... make an ass of itself. Probably the brightest thing that would occur to it to do would be to roll over on the ground, trot to the manger and start braying.

Dear Jesus, you too should say to him, **you have made me be your little donkey. Please don't leave me and I will stay with you always. Lead me, tightly harnessed by your grace. You have led me by the halter; make me do your Will. And so I will love you for ever and ever!**

The Forge, No. 381

Lord, here I am. It's up to you!'

Friends of God, No. 253

We will be able to keep going ahead, if only we seek our fortitude in him who says: 'Come to me all you who labor and are burdened and I will give you rest.' **Thank you, Lord, *quia tu es, Deus, fortitudo mea*, because you, and you alone, my God, have always been my strength, my refuge and my support.**

Friends of God, No. 131

" ... seeing a fig tree by the wayside he went up to it."

How wonderful, Lord, to see you hungry! To see you thirsty, too, by the well of Sichar! I contemplate you who are truly God, yet truly man, with flesh like my flesh.

'He emptied himself, taking the form of a slave,' so that I should never have the slightest doubt that he understands me and loves me.

Friends of God, No. 201

Sometimes, when things turn out the very opposite of what we intended, we cry out spontaneously: **Lord, it's all going wrong, every single thing I'm doing!** The time has come for us to rectify our approach and say: **With you, Lord, I will make steady headway, because you are strength itself.**

Friends of God, No. 213

Repeat to yourself, with all your heart, and with ever-increasing love, and more when you are in front of the Tabernacle or have the Lord within your breast: **"No one can hide from his warmth." May I not flee from you, may I be filled with the fire of your Holy Spirit.**

The Forge, No. 515

Lord, how useless I am, what a coward I have been! How many mistakes I've made, over and over again. And we can go further and say: **It's good, Lord, you have kept me up with your hand; for, left to myself, I am capable of the most disgraceful things. Don't let me go; keep on treating me as a little child. I want to be strong and brave and manly. But you must help me. I am a clumsy creature. Take me by the hand, Lord, and make sure your Mother is also by my side to guard me. And so, *possumus!* We can; we will be able to have you as our model.**

Christ is Passing By, No. 15

Heart on Fire

> The apostolic concern which burns in the heart of ordinary Christians is not something separate from their everyday work. It is part and parcel of one's work, which becomes a source of opportunities for meeting Christ. As we work at our job, side by side with our colleagues, friends and relatives, and sharing their interests, we can help them come closer to Christ.
>
> *Friends of God,* No. 264

Bringing those around me closer to God is the great ambition of the man or woman set on making Christ present in the world.

ꕥ

Help me to cry: **Jesus, souls! Apostolic souls! They are for you, for your glory.** You'll see how in the end he will hear us.

The Way, No. 804

Lord, we are glad to find ourselves in your wounded palm. Grasp us tight, squeeze us hard, make us lose all our earthly wretchedness, purify us, set us on fire, make us feel drenched in your Blood.

And then, cast us far, far away, hungry for the harvest, to sow the seed more fruitfully each day, for Love of you.

The Forge, No. 5

Jesus: wherever you have passed no heart remains indifferent. You are either loved or hated. When an apostle follows you, carrying out his duty, is it surprising that, if he is another Christ, he should arouse similar murmurs of aversion or of love?

The Way, No. 687

O Jesus…, strengthen our souls, open out the way for us, and, above all, intoxicate us with your Love! Make us into blazing fires to kindle the earth with the heavenly fire you brought us.

The Forge, No. 31

Dear Jesus: if I have to be an apostle, you will need to make me very humble.

May I know myself: may I know myself and know you. I will then never lose sight of my nothingness.

Furrow, No. 273

Cheer up!... Not least when the going gets hard. Doesn't it make you happy to think that your faithfulness to your Christian commitments depends to a large extent on you?

Be full of joy and freely renew your decision: **Lord, I want it too. Count on the little I have to offer.**

The Forge, No. 361

Make me into a saint, my God, even if you have to beat me into it. I don't want to be a hindrance to your Will. I want to respond, I want to be generous... But what sort of wanting is mine?

The Forge, No. 391

Personal freedom, which I defend and will always defend with all my strength, leads me to ask with deep conviction, though I am well aware of my own weakness: **What do you want from me, Lord, so that I may freely do it?**

Friends of God, No. 26

You grew in the face of difficulties in the apostolate when you prayed: **Lord, You are the same as ever. Give me the faith of those men who knew how to correspond to your grace, who worked great miracles, real marvels, in your Name...** And you finished off: **I know that you will do it; but I also know that you want to be asked. You want to be sought out. You want us to knock hard at the doors of your Heart.**

At the end you renewed your resolve to persevere in humble and trusting prayer.

The Forge, No. 653

I want, Lord, to abandon the care of all my affairs into your generous hands.

Our Mother, your Mother, will have let you hear those words, now as in Cana: 'They have none!'

I believe in you, I hope in you, I love you, Jesus. I want nothing for myself: it's for them.

The Forge, No. 807

Lord, make us crazy, with that infectious craziness that will draw many to your apostolate.

The Way, No. 916

When you open the Holy Gospel, think that what is written there — the words and deeds of Christ — is something that you should not only know, but live. Everything, every point that is told there, has been gathered, detail by detail, for you to make it come alive in the individual circumstances of your life.

You too, like the Apostle, will learn to ask, full of love, **"Lord, what would you have me do?..."** And in your soul you will hear the conclusive answer, "The Will of God!"

Take up the Gospel every day, then, and read it and live it as a definite rule. This is what the saints have done.

The Forge, No. 754

'Lord, I do believe! I have been brought up to believe in you. I have decided to follow you closely. Repeatedly during my life I have implored your mercy. And repeatedly too I have thought it impossible that you could perform such marvels in the hearts of your children. Lord, I do believe, but help me to believe more and better!'

Friends of God, No. 204

I look at your Cross, my Jesus, and I rejoice in your grace, because your Calvary has won for us the reward of the Holy Spirit. And you give yourself to me, each day, lovingly, madly, in the Sacred Host. And you have made me a son of God, and have given me your Mother to be mine.

I can't be satisfied with just giving thanks. My thoughts take flight: Lord, Lord, there are so many souls who are so far from you!

Foster those yearnings for apostolate in your life, that many may get to know him..., and love him..., and come to feel loved by him!

The Forge, No. 27

Part II

Words of the New Testament Meditated on Repeatedly

Words of the New Testament Meditated on Repeatedly

> Do you want to learn from Christ and follow the example of his life? Open the Holy Gospels and listen to God in dialogue with men… with you
>
> *Forge,* No. 322

As any reader of his homilies notices, St. Josemaría drew deeply from Holy Scripture in his preaching and writing. While reading the Gospel or praying the Liturgy of the Hours, he would jot down passages that he found helpful for his own prayer and preaching on small pieces of paper that he always carried with him.[9]

He drew together a large number of these notes on pages that were stapled together with a cover page reading "Words of the New Testament meditated on repeatedly, June, 1933." [10] It was a difficult time in the life of St. Josemaría and Opus Dei. The document was composed between the original publication of *Consideraciones Espirituales* in 1932 and the second edition published later in the summer of 1933. These were the predecessors of his spiritual classic, The Way.

Every passage of the New Testament has an intrinsic value, and many that opened wide horizons for St. Josemaría's interior life – such as the Nativity and Passion narratives - are not found here.

---

[9] For an in-depth description of St. Josemaría's use of these pieces of paper, see the introduction of Pedro Rodriguez, THE WAY, CRITICAL-HISTORICAL EDITION, London, Scepter, 2009, pp. 39-51.

[10] It was obviously his intention to transcribe these passages in the standard order of the New Testament books; but this discipline is interrupted at the 91st passage. The passages from 98 to the end were added after the initial transcription. The work was done by hand by a very busy man without the aid of a typewriter (not to mention a modern word-processing program). He obviously decided to add the 18 passages without rewriting the entire document. The document is an interesting testimony that St. Josemaría, who preached the importance of "finishing things well" had no mania of perfectionism.

Nevertheless, this collection teaches us that St. Josemaría "did not read the New Testament as something from another time but something through which he contemplated his personal life in the world around him. He regarded the sacred text as a point of reference to evaluate his own experience in its proper supernatural dimensions."[11]

> In our own life we must reproduce Christ's life. We need to come to know him by reading and meditating on Scripture, and by praying.[12]

In this collection of New Testament passages, originally handwritten in Latin, we can savor sources of prayer that St. Josemaría had personally selected, already meditated on, knew well and would use frequently in the years to come. Following some passages, St. Josemaría made marginal notes which are included below in italics.

It is also in this light that St. Josemaría can teach us to pray. But resist the temptation to skip around during a sitting. Repeat each passage over and over using your intellect, imagination and heart and let the Holy Spirit go to work.

---

[11] Varo, p. 274.
[12] CHRIST IS PASSING BY, No. 14.

Palabras del Nuevo testamento, repetidas veces meditadas. Junio-1933.

1—Facite ergo fructum dignum pœnitentiæ (Math, 3, 8 - San Juan a los fariseos)

2—Venite post me [si quis vult post me venire - -], et faciam vos fieri piscatores hominum (Math. 4, 19 - Jesús a Pedro y Andrés.)

3—Et tu Capharnaum, numquid usque in cælum exaltaberis? usque in infernum descendes; quia, si in Sodomis factæ fuis-sent virtutes, quæ factæ sunt in te, forte mansissent usque in hanc diem (Math. 11, 23 - abuso de las gracias.)

4—Dico autem vobis quoniam omne verbum otiosum, quod locuti fuerint homines, reddent rationem de eo in die judicii. Ex verbis enim tuis justificaberis, et ex verbis tuis condemnaberis. (Math. 12, 36 y 37)

5—Quæ est mater mea et quæ sunt fratres mei? Et exten-dens manus in discipulos suos, dixit: ecce mater mea et fra-tres mei. Quicumque enim fecerit voluntatem Patris mei, qui in cælis est: ipse meus frater, et soror, et mater est. (Math, 12, 48-50).

A portion of the first page of the document.

1 Bear fruit that befits repentance

Mt 3:8, *St John to the Pharisees*

2 And he said to them, "Follow me ["If any man would come after me", Mt 16:24], and I will make you fishers of men."

Mt 4:19, *Jesus to Peter and Andrew*

3 And you, Caper'na-um, will you be exalted to heaven? You shall be brought down to Hades. For if the mighty works done in you had been done in Sodom, it would have remained until this day.

Mt 11:23, *Abuse of graces*

4 I tell you, on the day of judgment men will render account for every careless word they utter; for by your words you will be justified, and by your words you will be condemned.

Mt 12:36-37

5 But he replied to the man who told him, "Who is my mother, and who are my brethren?" And stretching out his hand toward his disciples, he said, "Here are my mother and my brethren! For whoever does the will of my Father in heaven is my brother, and sister, and mother."

Mt 12:48-50

6 Why do your disciples transgress the tradition of the elders? For they do not wash their hands when they eat. You hypocrites! Well did Isaiah prophesy of you, when he said: 'This people honors me with their lips, but their heart is far from me."

Mt 15:2 and 7-8, *The scribes and Pharisees and Jesus' reply*

7 He answered, "Every plant which my heavenly Father has not planted will be rooted up. Let them alone; they are blind guides. And if a blind man leads a blind man, both will fall into a pit."

Mt 15:13-14

8 Again I say to you, if two of you agree on earth about anything they ask, it will be done for them by my Father in heaven. For where two or three are gathered in my name, there am I in the midst of them.

Mt 18:19-20

9 For there are eunuchs who have been so from birth, and there are eunuchs who have been made eunuchs by men, and there are eunuchs who have made themselves eunuchs for the sake of the kingdom of heaven. He who is able to receive this, let him receive it.

Mt 19:12

10 And about the eleventh hour he went out and found others standing; and he said to them, "Why do you stand here idle all day?" They said to him, "Because no one has hired us." He said to them, "You go into the vineyard too."

Mt 20:6-7, *Mt 20:16 the last will be first, and the first last.*

11 Whoever would be first among you must be your slave; even as the Son of man came not to be served but to serve, and to give his life as a ransom for many.

Mt 20: 27-28

12 "Whoever receives one such child in my name receives me; and whoever receives me, receives not me but him who sent me." John said to him, "Teacher, we saw a man casting out demons in your name, and we forbade him, because he was not following us." But Jesus said, "Do not forbid him; for no one who does a mighty work in my name will be able soon after to speak evil of me".

Mk 9:37-39

13 Salt is good; but if the salt has lost its saltiness, how will you season it? Have salt in yourselves, and be at peace with one another.

Mk 9:50

14 Jesus was walking ahead of them; and they were amazed, and those who followed were afraid.

Mk 10:32, *Christ thirsts to suffer on the Cross in Jerusalem*

15 Truly, I say to you, whoever says to this mountain, 'Be taken up and cast into the sea,' and does not doubt in his heart, but believes that what he says will come to pass, it will be done for him. Therefore I tell you, whatever you ask in prayer, believe that you receive it, and you will.

Mk 11:23-24

16 In truth, I tell you, there were many widows in Israel in the days of Eli'jah, when the heaven was shut up three years and six months, when there came a great famine over all the land; and Eli'jah was sent to none of them but only to Zar'ephath, in the land of Sidon, to a woman who was a widow. And there were many lepers in Israel in the time of the prophet Eli'sha; and none of them was cleansed, but only Na'aman the Syrian."

Lk 4:25-27

17 And he came and touched the bier, and the bearers stood still. And he said, "Young man, I say to you, arise." And the dead man sat up, and began to speak. And he gave him to his mother.

Lk 7:14-15, *Resurrection of the son of the widow of Naim*

18 "Truly I tell you, this poor widow has put in more than all of them."

Lk 21:3

19 They said to each other, "Did not our hearts burn within us while he talked to us on the road, while he opened to us the scriptures?"

Lk 24:32, *The disciples of Emmaus*

20 The wind blows where it wills…

Jn 3:8, *Chat with Nicodemus*

21 Jesus said to them, "My food is to do the will of him who sent me, and to accomplish his work.

Jn 4:34

22 Sir, I have no man…

Jn 5:7, *At the Probatic Pool in Jerusalem*

23 After this many of his disciples drew back and no longer went about with him. Jesus said to the twelve, "Will you also go away?" Simon Peter answered him, "Lord, to whom shall we go? You have the words of eternal life; and we have believed, and have come to know, that you are the Holy One of God."

Jn 6:66-69

24 He who is of God hears the words of God; the reason why you do not hear them is that you are not of God.

Jn 8:47, *To the Pharisees*

25 We know that God does not listen to sinners, but if any one is a worshiper of God and does his will, God listens to him.

Jn 9:31, *Response of the man born blind to the Pharisees*

26 Jesus said, "For judgment I came into this world, that those who do not see may see, and that those who see may become blind."

Jn 9:39, *Follows Jn 9:38 "Lord, I believe"; and he worshiped him.*

27 My sheep hear my voice, and I know them, and they follow me; and I give them eternal life, and they shall never perish, and no one shall snatch them out of my hand. My Father, who has given them to me, is greater than all, and no one is able to snatch them out of the Father's hand.

Jn 10:27-29

28 Jesus wept.

Jn 11:35, *Death of Lazarus*

29 A new commandment I give to you, that you love one another; even as I have loved you, that you also love one another. By this all men will know that you are my disciples, if you have love for one another.

Jn 13:34-35

30 I will not leave you desolate; I will come to you.

Jn 14:18

31 I am the vine, you are the branches. He who abides in me, and I in him, he it is that bears much fruit, for apart from me you can do nothing.

Jn 15:5

32 Abide in me, and I in you. As the branch cannot bear fruit by itself, unless it abides in the vine, neither can you, unless you abide in me.

Jn 15:4

33 If you abide in me, and my words abide in you, ask whatever you will, and it shall be done for you.

Jn 15:7

34 I have given them thy word; and the world has hated them because they are not of the world, even as I am not of the world. I do not pray that thou shouldst take them out of the world, but that thou shouldst keep them from the evil one. They are not of the world, even as I am not of the world. Sanctify them in the truth; thy word is truth.

Jn 17:14-17, *I would willingly copy to the end of the chapter*

35 I have said this to you, that in me you may have peace. In the world you have tribulation; but be of good cheer, I have overcome the world.

Jn 16:33, *Jesus says this after saying: The hour is coming, indeed it has come, when you will be scattered, every man to his home, and will leave me alone; yet I am not alone, for the Father is with me.*

36 And now I am no more in the world, but they are in the world, and I am coming to thee. Holy Father, keep them in thy name, which thou hast given me, that they may be one, even as we are one.

Jn 17:11, *He prays for his disciples and for the Church [ut omnes unum sint] after having prayed for Himself*

37 Now Judas, who betrayed him, also knew the place; for Jesus often met there with his disciples.

Jn 18:2

38 Jesus answered, "I told you that I am he; so, if you seek me, let these men go." This was to fulfill the word which he had spoken, "Of those whom you gave me I lost not one."

Jn 18:8-9

39 Peter stood outside at the door. So the other disciple, who was known to the high priest, went out and spoke to the maid who kept the door, and brought Peter in.

Jn 18:16

40 Jesus said to her, "Do not hold me, for I have not yet ascended to the Father; but go to my brethren and say to them, I am ascending to my Father and your Father, to my God and your God."

Jn 20:17, *On appearing to Mary Magdalene*

41 This is the stone which was rejected by you builders, but which has become the head of the corner.

Acts 4:11, *Peter to the leaders and elders of the people who had arrested him with John after they cured the man blind from birth." I have no silver and gold, but I give you what I have; in the name of Jesus Christ of Nazareth, walk." Acts 3:6*

42 Whether it is right in the sight of God to listen to you rather than to God, you must judge; for we cannot but speak of what we have seen and heard.

Acts 4:19-20, *Response of Peter to the Sanhedrin*

43 It is not right that we should give up preaching the word of God to serve tables… pick out from among you seven men of good repute, full of the Spirit and of wisdom, whom we may appoint to this duty. We will devote ourselves to prayer and to the ministry of the word.

Acts 6:2-4

44 And the believers from among the circumcised who came with Peter were amazed, because the gift of the Holy Spirit had been poured out even on the Gentiles.

Acts 10:45, *Conversion of Cornelius*

45 If you live according to the flesh you will die, but if by the Spirit you put to death the deeds of the body you will live.

Rom 8:13

46 If children, then heirs, heirs of God and fellow heirs with Christ, provided we suffer with him in order that we may also be glorified with him.

Rom 8:17

47 And those whom he predestined he also called; and those whom he called he also justified; and those whom he justified he also glorified.

Rom 8:30

48 Who shall separate us from the love of Christ? Shall tribulation, or distress, or persecution, or famine, or nakedness, or peril, or sword? As it is written, "For thy sake we are being killed all the day long; we are regarded as sheep to be slaughtered." No, in all these things we are more than conquerors through him who loved us. For I am sure that neither death, nor life, nor angels, nor principalities, nor things present, nor things to come, nor powers, nor height, nor depth, nor anything else in all creation, will be able to separate us from the love of God in Christ Jesus our Lord.

Rom 8:35-39

49 For Jews demand signs and Greeks seek wisdom, but we preach Christ crucified, a stumbling block to Jews and folly to Gentiles.

1 Cor 1:22-23

50 For consider your call, brethren; not many of you were wise according to worldly standards, not many were powerful, not many were of noble birth; but God chose what is foolish in the world to shame the wise, God chose what is weak in the world to shame the strong, God chose what is low and despised in the world, even things that are not, to bring to nothing things that are, so that no human being might boast in the presence of God… therefore, as it is written, "Let him who boasts, boast of the Lord."

1 Cor 1:26-29 & 30

51 For I decided to know nothing among you except Jesus Christ and him crucified.

1 Cor 2:2

52 Do you not know that you are God's temple and that God's Spirit dwells in you?

1 Cor 3:16

53 Let no one deceive himself. If any one among you thinks that he is wise in this age, let him become a fool that he may become wise.

1 Cor 3:18

54 So let no one boast of men. For all things are yours…

1 Cor 3:21

55 For the wisdom of this world is folly with God. For it is written, "He catches the wise in their craftiness," and again, "The Lord knows that the thoughts of the wise are futile."

1 Cor 3:19-20

56 For neither circumcision counts for anything nor uncircumcision, but keeping the commandments of God.

1 Cor 7:19

57 For if I preach the gospel, that gives me no ground for boasting. For necessity is laid upon me. Woe to me if I do not preach the gospel!

1 Cor 9:16

58 But I pommel my body and subdue it, lest after preaching to others I myself should be disqualified.

1 Cor 9:27

59 Therefore let any one who thinks that he stands take heed lest he fall.

1 Cor 10:12, *Bad example of Israelites serve as an example to the Corinthians*

60 So, whether you eat or drink, or whatever you do, do all to the glory of God.

1 Cor 10:31

61 If one member suffers, all suffer together; if one member is honored, all rejoice together.

1 Cor 12:26

62 If I speak in the tongues of men and of angels, but have not love, I am a noisy gong or a clanging cymbal. Etc.

1 Cor 13:1, *The whole chapter*

63 For I through the law died to the law, that I might live to God. I have been crucified with Christ; it is no longer I who live, but Christ who lives in me; and the life I now live in the flesh I live by faith in the Son of God, who loved me and gave himself for me.

Gal 2:19-20

64 My little children, with whom I am again in travail until Christ be formed in you!

Gal 4:19

65 Bear one another's burdens, and so fulfil the law of Christ.

Gal 6:2

66 And walk in love, as Christ loved us and gave himself up for us, a fragrant offering and sacrifice to God.

Eph 5:2

67 Complete my joy by being of the same mind, having the same love, being in full accord and of one mind.

Phil 2:2

68 Let each of you look not only to his own interests, but also to the interests of others.

Phil 2:4

69 That you may be blameless and innocent, children of God without blemish in the midst of a crooked and perverse generation, among whom you shine as lights in the world.

Phil 2:15

70 See to it that no one makes a prey of you by philosophy and empty deceit, according to human tradition, according to the elemental spirits of the universe, and not according to Christ.

Col 2:8

71 If then you have been raised with Christ, seek the things that are above, where Christ is, seated at the right hand of God. Set your minds on things that are above, not on things that are on earth.

Col 3:1-2

72 … seeing that you have put off the old nature with its practices.

Col 3:9

73 Let your speech always be gracious, seasoned with salt, so that you may know how you ought to answer every one.

Col 4:6, *After warning: Conduct yourselves wisely toward outsiders*

74 But concerning love of the brethren you have no need to have any one write to you, for you yourselves have been taught by God to love one another.

1 Thes 4:9

75 Therefore encourage one another and build one another up, just as you are doing.

1 Thes 5:11

76 He who calls you is faithful, and he will do it.

1 Thes 5:24

77 I thank him who has given me strength for this, Christ Jesus our Lord, because he judged me faithful by appointing me to his service.

1 Tim 1:12

78 If any of you lacks wisdom, let him ask God, who gives to all men generously and without reproaching, and it will be given him.

James 1:5

79 Blessed is the man who endures trial, for when he has stood the test he will receive the crown of life which God has promised to those who love him.

James 1:12

80 But be doers of the word, and not hearers only, deceiving yourselves.

James 1:22

81 What does it profit, my brethren, if a man says he has faith but has not works? Can his faith save him?

James 2:14

82 Therefore confess your sins to one another, and pray for one another, that you may be healed. The prayer of a righteous man has great power in its effects. Eli'jah was a man of like nature with ourselves and he prayed fervently that it might not rain, and for three years and six months it did not rain on the earth.

James 5:16-17

83 Having purified your souls by your obedience to the truth for a sincere love of the brethren, love one another earnestly from the heart.

1 Ptr 1:22

84 For you have tasted the kindness of the Lord.

1 Ptr 2:3

85 Above all hold unfailing your love for one another, since love covers a multitude of sins.

1 Ptr 4:8

86 But do not ignore this one fact, beloved, that with the Lord one day is as a thousand years, and a thousand years as one day.

2 Ptr 3:8

87 Do not wonder, brethren, that the world hates you. We know that we have passed out of death into life, because we love the brethren. He who does not love remains in death.

1 Jn 3:13-14

88 Little children, let us not love in word or speech but in deed and in truth.

1 Jn 3:18

89 Beloved, if God so loved us, we also ought to love one another.

1 Jn 4:11

90 For whatever is born of God overcomes the world; and this is the victory that overcomes the world, our faith.

1 Jn 5:4

91 It is better for you to enter life maimed or lame than with two hands or two feet to be thrown into the eternal fire.

Matt 18:8

92 We brought nothing into the world, and we cannot take anything out of the world.

1 Tim 6:7

93 No one can serve two masters; for either he will hate the one and love the other, or he will be devoted to the one and despise the other. You cannot serve God and mammon.

Matt 6:24

94 And to the angel of the church in La-odice'a write: "The words of the Amen, the faithful and true witness, the beginning of God's creation. I know your works: you are neither cold nor hot. Would that you were cold or hot! So, because you are lukewarm, and neither cold nor hot, I will spew you out of my mouth."

Rev 3:14-16

95 Those whom I love, I reprove and chasten; so be zealous and repent.

Rev 3:19

96 Behold, I stand at the door and knock; if any one hears my voice and opens the door, I will come in to him and eat with him, and he with me.

Rev 3:20

97 He who conquers, I will grant him to sit with me on my throne, as I myself conquered and sat down with my Father on his throne.

Rev 3:21

98 In these last days he has spoken to us by a Son, whom he appointed the heir of all things, through whom also he created the world.

Heb 1:2

99 But who are you, a man, to answer back to God? Will what is molded say to its molder, "Why have you made me thus?" Has the potter no right over the clay, to make out of the same lump one vessel for beauty and another for menial use?

Rom 9:20-21

100 For the Son of man came to seek and to save the lost.

Lk 19:10

101 "Put out into the deep and let down your nets for a catch." *Peter says they haven't caught any fish the whole night and now* "when they had done this, they enclosed a great shoal of fish", and Peter said "Depart from me, for I am a sinful man, O Lord." And Jesus: "Do not be afraid; henceforth you will be catching men." And when they had brought their boats to land, they left everything and followed him.

Lk 5:4, 6,8,10-11

102 They said to him, "Every one is searching for you"... He had cured Peter's mother-in-law and had healed many others from sickness and demons. And in the morning, a great while before day, he rose and went out to a lonely place, and there he prayed.

Mk 1:37 & 35, *Peter is following him along with others when Peter says the phrase above.*

103 And he said to them, "Come away by yourselves to a lonely place, and rest a while." For many were coming and going, and they had no leisure even to eat.

Mk 6:31, *The Apostles return from their first apostolic outing full of enthusiasm, enamored of their vocation by the success obtained Then Jesus takes them out to the desert, without food. Many people follow him and he gives them something to eat with 5 loaves and 2 fish (5000 men and 12 baskets of leftovers).*

104 And there was a woman who had had a spirit of infirmity for eighteen years; she was bent over and could not fully straighten herself. And when Jesus saw her, he called her and said to her, "Woman, you are freed from your infirmity." And he laid his hands upon her, and immediately she was made straight, and she praised God.

Lk 13:11-13, *How many bent and twisted souls!*

105 At that very hour some Pharisees came, and said to him, "Get away from here, for Herod wants to kill you."

Lk 13:31, *Before finishing the parables of the mustard seed, the leaven and the narrow gate. And he answers the Pharisees:*

106 Go and tell that fox, "Behold, I cast out demons and perform cures today and tomorrow, and the third day I finish my course."

Lk 13:32, *So he would speak to today's politicians.*

107 "Increase our faith!"

Lk 17:5, *He tells of the scandals to come (the millstone) and then of how many times to pardon the repentant sinner, when the apostles ask.*

108 Jesus wept.

Jn 11:35, *Resurrection of Lazarus*

109 Some of them went to the Pharisees and told them what Jesus had done.

Jn 11:46, *After Lazarus rises, the Jews inform and the Pharisees form a Council.*

110 So the chief priests and the Pharisees gathered the council, and said, "What are we to do? For this man performs many signs. If we let him go on thus, every one will believe in him, and the Romans will come and destroy both our holy place and our nation." But one of them, Ca'iaphas, who was high priest that year, said to them, "You know nothing at all; you do not understand that it is expedient for you that one man should die for the people, and that the whole nation should not perish." So from that day on they took counsel how to put him to death.

Jn 11:47-50 & 53

111 Take my yoke upon you, and learn from me; for I am gentle and lowly in heart, and you will find rest for your souls.

Matt 11:29

And those who are in the flesh cannot please God.

Rom 8:8

Made in United States
North Haven, CT
31 March 2022